The Michigan Wolverines

BY
MARK STEWART

NORWOOD HOUSE PRESS

CHICAGO, ILLINOIS

Norwood House Paperback Editions
An Imprint of Norwood House Press
P.O. Box 316598
Chicago, Illinois 60631

For information regarding Norwood House Press, please visit our website at:
www.norwoodhousepress.com or call 866-565-2900.

All photos courtesy of Icon SMI except the following:
Topps, Inc. (6, 16, 20); Time Inc./Sports Illustrated (7); Classic Games (9, 21);
Author's Collection (14, 30, 36, 37 top, 40 bottom); The Associated Press (17, 18, 19, 26, 29, 31 & 33);
TK Legacy, Inc. (22, 24, 37 bottom left, 40 top left); University of Michigan (28);
SA•GE Collectibles, Inc. (37 bottom right, 40 bottom left); First of America (41).

Cover Photo: Donald Miralle/Getty Images

Special thanks to Topps, Inc.

Editor: Mike Kennedy
Designer: Ron Jaffe
Project Management: Black Book Partners, LLC.
Research: Joshua Zaffos

The Library of Congress has cataloged the original hardcover edition as follows:

Stewart, Mark, 1960-
  The Michigan Wolverines / by Mark Stewart.
      p. cm. -- (Team spirit college football)
  Includes bibliographical references and index.
  Summary: "Presents the history and accomplishments of the University of
Michigan Wolverines football team. Includes highlights of players, coaches
and awards, longstanding rivalries, quotes, timelines, maps, glossary and
websites"--Provided by publisher.
  ISBN-13: 978-1-59953-278-3 (library edition : alk. paper)
  ISBN-10: 1-59953-278-6 (library edition : alk. paper) 1. Michigan
Wolverines (Football team)--History--Juvenile literature. 2. University of
Michigan--Football--History--Juvenile literature. I. Title.
  GV958.U52863S74 2009
  796.332'630977435--dc22
                                                        2008037511

COVER PHOTO: The Wolverines get ready to take the field before the 2004 Rose Bowl.

Table of Contents

CHAPTER	PAGE
Meet the Wolverines	4
Way Back When	6
21st Century	10
Home Turf	12
Dressed for Success	14
We're Number 1!	16
Go-To Guys: Trophy Case	20
Go-To Guys: Game Breakers	22
Go-To Guys: Impact Players	24
On the Sidelines	26
Rivals	28
One Great Day	30
It Really Happened	32
Team Spirit	34
Timeline	36
Fun Facts	38
For the Record	40
The Big Ten	42
The College Game	44
Glossary	46
Places to Go	47
Index	48

SPORTS WORDS & VOCABULARY WORDS: In this book, you will find many words that are new to you. You may also see familiar words used in new ways. The glossary on page 46 gives the meanings of football words, as well as "everyday" words that have special football meanings. These words appear in **bold type** throughout the book. The glossary on page 47 gives the meanings of vocabulary words that are not related to football. They appear in ***bold italic type*** throughout the book.

Meet the Wolverines

In the fast-moving world of college sports, it is good to know that a handful of schools still win the old-fashioned way. The University of Michigan Wolverines have been **blocking** and tackling their opponents—and doing it with great success—for more than 125 years. A player from today's squad would probably fit right into a team practice from 50 or 100 years ago. The Wolverines from those *eras* would feel right at home today.

Michigan's winning attitude has never changed, either. The Wolverines play in the Big Ten Conference and have won the conference title more than 40 times. They have been crowned national champions 10 times.

This book tells the story of the Wolverines. With each victory, Michigan's amazing football history grows. Today's players are part of that line of success. Their challenge is not just winning games—it is upholding the school's famous team spirit and *traditions*.

Michigan players race onto their home field before a 2002 game. Touching the "GO BLUE" banner is one of the team's great traditions.

Way Back When

HARRY NEWMAN Quarterback
MICHIGAN
ALL AMERICAN

Michigan has been playing football since 1879. During the 1880s, the school helped make the sport very popular in the country's midsection. By the early 1900s, no college team could compare with the Wolverines. Coach Fielding Yost taught his players to keep the pressure on opponents all game long. From 1901 to 1905, Michigan went 55–1–1. In 1901, the Wolverines outscored their opponents 550–0!

Yost won six national championships. His last came in 1923. That team starred Harry Kipke and Jack Blott. Kipke later became Michigan's coach. One of his best players was Harry Newman, who was named college football's **Most Valuable Player (MVP)** in 1932. From 1930 to 1933, the Wolverines lost only one game.

During the late 1930s and early 1940s, Michigan fans cheered for Tom Harmon, the most exciting player in college football. In 1940, Harmon won the **Heisman Trophy**. He nearly led Michigan to another national championship that season.

In 1947 and 1948, the Wolverines were unbeaten. They played a whirling, swirling offense that confused opponents. Often, defenders would tackle one or two Michigan players only to find that another actually had the ball! Those teams were nicknamed the "Mad Magicians." The 1948 Wolverines won the national championship.

During the 1950s and 1960s, Michigan competed with Michigan State University to see which school was the best in the state. The

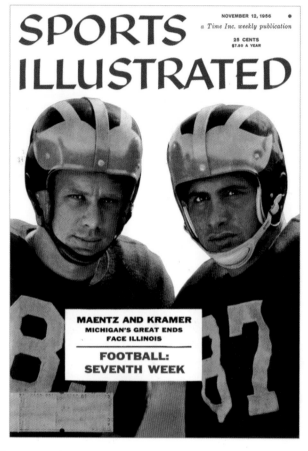

SPORTS ILLUSTRATED

NOVEMBER 12, 1956

a Time Inc. weekly publication

25 CENTS
$7.50 A YEAR

MAENTZ AND KRAMER
MICHIGAN'S GREAT ENDS
FACE ILLINOIS

FOOTBALL:
SEVENTH WEEK

Wolverines had many good players during those years, including Ron Kramer, Tom Maentz, Bob Timberlake, Bill Yearby, Tom Mack, Rick Volk, and Ron Johnson. The 1964 team came within one victory of another national championship.

The Wolverines of the 1970s were coached by Bo Schembechler. The 1971 team went 11–0 before losing by one point in the **Rose Bowl**. That squad was led by a great offensive line. In 1976, running

LEFT: Harry Newman, a star for Michigan in the 1930s.
ABOVE: Tom Maentz and Ron Kramer are featured on this 1956 *Sports Illustrated* cover. Michigan fans loved to read about their favorite players in magazines and newspapers.

back Rob Lytle, quarterback Rick Leach, and linebacker Calvin O'Neal helped Michigan rise to #3 in the nation.

Over the next 20 years, many good players wore the blue and maize, including Anthony Carter, Jim Harbaugh, Jumbo Elliott, and Desmond Howard, who won the Heisman Trophy in 1991. However, not until 1997 did Michigan finish the year again as the top college team.

Desmond Howard
WR

That season, quarterback Brian Griese and defensive back Charles Woodson led the Wolverines to a perfect 12–0 record. They beat Big Ten **rival** Ohio State University in the last game of the season. Next, they defeated Washington State University in the Rose Bowl to win the national championship.

Michigan shared that title with the University of Nebraska. Both schools were **undefeated**. Many college football fans were annoyed that the two best teams didn't play each other. That would soon change. Since 1998, the #1 and #2 teams in the rankings have played in the title game of the **Bowl Championship Series (BCS)**. Every year, Michigan fans root hard for their Wolverines to be one of those clubs.

LEFT: Charles Woodson scans the field. In 1997, he became the third Wolverine to win the Heisman Trophy.
ABOVE: Desmond Howard, the second Wolverine to win the Heisman.

21st Century

After winning the national championship in 1997, the Wolverines set a new goal. They wanted to capture their first national championship of the 21st *century*. They won or shared the Big Ten championship in four of the next seven seasons, thanks to players such as Chris Perry, Braylon Edwards, David Baas, and LaMarr Woodley.

Michigan finished in the Top 20 almost every year after 1997, but the team fell short of the national championship each season. Still, the Wolverines continued to produce stars who were **drafted** by the **National Football League (NFL)**. In fact, today it is hard to find a **professional** team without a Michigan player on its **roster**.

To reach the top of college football again, Michigan hired Rich Rodriguez to coach the team in 2008. Rodriguez was known for his *imaginative* plays on offense. Combined with Michigan's famous defense, the team's high-flying offense made the Wolverines even more exciting to watch. Fans looked forward to a new era of success in Ann Arbor.

Jake Long, Chad Henne, and Mike Hart pose for a photo before the 2007 season. They all moved on to the NFL the following year.

Home Turf

The home for Michigan's first football teams was known as the Ann Arbor Fairgrounds. As the school's games drew more and more fans, the Wolverines moved to Regents Field and later Ferry Field. By the 1920s, Michigan needed a modern stadium.

In 1927, Michigan Stadium opened. At the time, it held more than 70,000 fans—and was built to keep growing. Since the mid-1970s, more than 100,000 fans have jammed into the stadium for every game. The Wolverines lead the nation in attendance almost every year. That's one reason that Michigan Stadium is known as the "Big House."

BY THE NUMBERS

- *There are 107,501 seats for football at Michigan Stadium.*
- *Michigan beat Ohio Wesleyan University 33–0 in the first game at Michigan Stadium.*
- *As of 2008, Michigan had retired five jersey numbers—98 (Tom Harmon), 87 (Ron Kramer), 48 (Gerald Ford), 47 (Bennie Oosterbaan), and 11 (The Wistert Brothers—Albert, Alvin, and Francis).*

Fans cheer on the Wolverines during a 2006 game at Michigan Stadium.

Dressed for Success

Michigan has been playing football since the 1870s. The team's colors have been around even longer. In 1867, a group of students picked yellow and blue as the official school colors. The bright shade of yellow is called maize, which is another name for corn. The team has been wearing blue uniforms since the 1920s. The Wolverines began wearing white uniforms for road games in 1949. The team added player names to the back of their jerseys in 1980.

BENNY
FRIEDMAN

The Michigan helmet might be the most famous in college football. The front has a wing design with three stripes. The Wolverines began using this style in 1938. Coach Fritz Crisler believed his quarterbacks would have an easier time spotting their receivers with a helmet that was easy to see. In 1938, Michigan doubled its passing yards and threw almost half as many **interceptions**.

This picture—which was pasted into a child's scrapbook from the 1920s—shows Benny Friedman in the Michigan uniform from that period.

UNIFORM BASICS

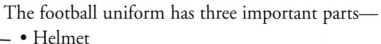

The football uniform has three important parts—

- Helmet
- Jersey
- Pants

Helmets used to be made out of leather, and they did not have facemasks—ouch! Today, helmets are made of super-strong plastic. The uniform top, or jersey, is made of thick fabric. It fits snugly around a player so that tacklers cannot grab it and pull him down. The pants come down just over the knees.

There is a lot more to a football uniform than what you see on the outside. Air can be pumped inside the helmet to give it a snug, padded fit. The jersey covers shoulder pads, and sometimes a rib protector called a flak jacket. The pants include pads that protect the hips, thighs, *tailbone*, and knees.

Football teams have two sets of uniforms—one dark and one light. This makes it easier to tell two teams apart on the field. Almost all teams wear their dark uniforms at home and their light ones on the road.

Mike Hart runs down the field in Michigan's 2007 home uniform.

We're Number 1!

The Wolverines were national champions each year from 1901 to 1904. They scored so easily that they forever became known as the "Point-A-Minute" teams. Coach Fielding Yost had four good runners in the same **backfield**. Harrison Weeks played quarterback, and Neil Snow was the fullback. The two halfbacks were Albert Herrnstein and Willie Heston.

MICHIGAN

ALL AMERICAN

WILLIE HESTON *Halfback*

Heston ran like a modern player at a time when the game was much slower. Once he made it through the first line of tacklers, no one could catch him. Heston scored 72 touchdowns during his Michigan career, and his teams never lost a game.

Michigan was crowned the national champ again in 1918 and 1923. The 1918 Wolverines played only five games because of World War I. The 1923 team, however, went 8–0. In five of those victories, Michigan did not allow a point.

Many fans felt that the 1947 Wolverines should have finished the season ranked #1. They were an exciting and talented team led by coach Fritz Crisler. The Wolverines had a record of 10–0 and beat the University of Southern California (USC) 49–0 in the Rose Bowl. Notre Dame University also went undefeated that year and was awarded the national championship before the Rose Bowl was played.

Crisler retired after the 1947 season. His replacement, Bennie Oosterbaan, had been a great player for Michigan in the 1920s. He guided the Wolverines to another undefeated season in 1948. Oosterbaan welcomed new stars such as quarterback Pete Elliott and end Dick Rifenburg. Michigan went 9–0 and gave up only 44 points.

After beating Ohio State in their last game, the Wolverines did not play in a bowl game. Conference rules at the time did not allow

LEFT: A trading card of Willie Heston, who made Michigan the nation's best team in the early 1900s.   **ABOVE**: Bob Chappuis breaks through a tackle during the 1948 Rose Bowl against USC.

schools to play in bowl games two years in a row. So Michigan got an early Christmas present—the national championship!

Nearly 50 years passed before Michigan returned to the top of college football. In 1997, the Wolverines had an amazing offense.

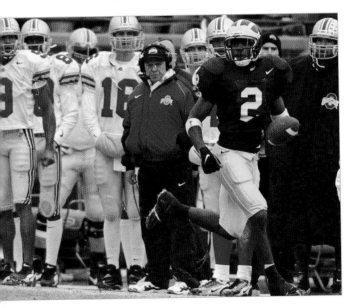

Quarterback Brian Griese led an attack that included running back Chris Howard and receivers Jerame Tuman and Tai Streets. The defense starred **sack** master Glen Steele and Charles Woodson in the **secondary**. The speedy Woodson—who also played on offense—had eight interceptions and won the Heisman Trophy.

Woodson had his best game against Ohio State. He intercepted a pass and scored a long touchdown on a punt return to give Michigan a 20–14 victory in the last game of the regular season.

The Wolverines then turned their attention to the Rose Bowl. Griese had a great game against Washington State University. With time running out, Michigan held a 21–16 lead. The Cougars wanted to try one last desperate play but the clock ran out. After 49 years, the Wolverines were national champions again.

ABOVE: Ohio State's players and coaches can only watch from the sidelines as Charles Woodson goes all the way on a punt return during the 1997 season. **RIGHT**: Brian Griese celebrates after Michigan's victory over Washington State in the Rose Bowl.

Go-To Guys

BENNY FRIEDMAN — Quarterback

ALL AMERICAN

BENNY FRIEDMAN   *Quarterback*

- BORN: 3/18/1905   • DIED: 11/23/1982
- PLAYED FOR VARSITY: 1924–1926

When Benny Friedman played for Michigan, the football was nine inches fatter than it is today. Friedman was one of the first players who could throw accurate passes. In 1926, he was voted the conference Player of the Year.

TOM HARMON — Running Back

- BORN: 9/28/1919   • DIED: 3/15/1990   • PLAYED FOR VARSITY: 1938–1940

Tom Harmon was a great runner and passer, tough blocker, talented kicker, and an excellent defender. Harmon led the nation in scoring in 1939 and 1940, and won the Heisman Trophy in 1940.

ANTHONY CARTER — Receiver

- BORN: 9/17/1960   • PLAYED FOR VARSITY: 1979–1982

Anthony Carter fueled Michigan's passing attack during the early 1980s. He was the first player from the Big Ten since the 1940s to be named **All-American** three years in a row. In 1982, he was voted the conference Player of the Year.

JIM HARBAUGH Quarterback

- BORN: 12/23/1963 • PLAYED FOR VARSITY: 1983–1986

During Jim Harbaugh's four years at Michigan, he gave the Wolverines a chance to win every time they took the field. Few players in team history could match his talent and *competitive* spirit. Harbaugh was named Big Ten Player of the Year in 1986.

DESMOND HOWARD Receiver/Kick Returner

- BORN: 5/15/1970
- PLAYED FOR VARSITY: 1989–1991

Every time Desmond Howard touched the ball, Michigan fans jumped out of their seats. He led the Big Ten with 138 points in 1991 and won several awards, including the Heisman Trophy.

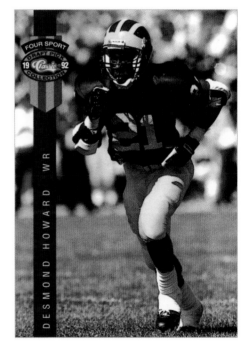

CHARLES WOODSON Defensive Back

- BORN: 10/7/1976
- PLAYED FOR VARSITY: 1995–1997

During Charles Woodson's three seasons at Michigan, few quarterbacks dared to throw the ball in his direction. In 1997, Woodson led the Wolverines to a share of the national championship and became the first defensive player to win the Heisman Trophy.

LEFT: Benny Friedman
RIGHT: Desmond Howard

WILLIE HESTON — Running Back

- BORN: 9/8/1878 • DIED: 9/9/1963 • PLAYED FOR VARSITY: 1901–1904

Willie Heston was fast and shifty. When he burst through the **line of scrimmage**, no one could catch him. Heston finished his career as the all-time leader in touchdowns for the Wolverines.

BENNIE OOSTERBAAN — Receiver/Defensive End

THE LEGEND OF
BENNIE OOSTERBAAN
Three-Time All-American

- BORN: 2/4/1906 • DIED: 10/25/1990
- PLAYED FOR VARSITY: 1925–1927

Bennie Oosterbaan was one of the greatest Wolverines of the 1920s. He was the best receiver in the Big Ten and one of the few players who could tackle the nation's best running back, Red Grange, without any help from a teammate.

BOB CHAPPUIS — Running Back

- BORN: 2/24/1923
- PLAYED FOR VARSITY: 1942 & 1946–1947

Bob Chappuis was a dangerous player. He could pass and run as well as anyone in the Big Ten. After time off because of World War II, Chappuis led the Wolverines to an undefeated season in 1947 and was runner-up for the Heisman Trophy.

ABOVE: Bennie Oosterbaan   **RIGHT**: Braylon Edwards

22

RICK LEACH   Quarterback

• BORN: 5/4/1957   • PLAYED FOR VARSITY: 1975–1978

Rick Leach was a great passer who played for a team that loved to run the football. Still, he broke Michigan records for passing yards and touchdowns. Leach led the Wolverines to three victories in a row over Ohio State.

BUTCH WOOLFOLK   Running Back

• BORN: 3/1/1960

• PLAYED FOR VARSITY: 1978–1981

Butch Woolfolk was a threat to go for a touchdown every time he touched the ball. Woolfolk topped the Wolverines in rushing three seasons in a row and graduated as the school's all-time leading runner. He set a Michigan record in 1979 with a 92-yard run for a touchdown.

BRAYLON EDWARDS   Receiver

• BORN: 2/21/1983

• PLAYED FOR VARSITY: 2001–2004

Braylon Edwards followed in his father's footsteps when he joined the Wolverines in 2001. Stan Edwards played for Michigan in the 1980s. In 2004, Braylon set a team record with 97 catches and was named Big Ten MVP.

ALVIN WISTERT — Lineman

- BORN: 6/26/1916 • DIED: 10/3/2005 • PLAYED FOR VARSITY: 1947–1949

Alvin Wistert signed a baseball contract with the Cincinnati Reds when he was 17, but he hurt his pitching arm. He later fought in World War II. When Wistert arrived at Michigan, he was a 30-year-old freshman. He and his brothers, Albert and Francis, were all Michigan legends.

RON KRAMER — Receiver

- BORN: 6/24/1935 • PLAYED FOR VARSITY: 1954–1956

Ron Kramer did it all for Michigan. He caught passes, kicked **field goals**, punted, and played linebacker. Kramer was also a great basketball player. He topped the football and basketball teams in scoring as a junior and senior.

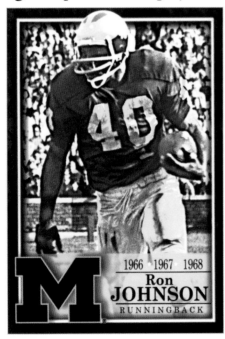

1966 1967 1968
Ron JOHNSON
RUNNINGBACK

RON JOHNSON — Running Back

- BORN: 10/17/1947
- PLAYED FOR VARSITY: 1965–1968

Ron Johnson split his time at Michigan between the football field and the engineering building. In 1968, he led an amazing ***comeback*** against the University of Wisconsin by running for 347 yards and five touchdowns.

REGGIE McKENZIE   Offensive Lineman

- BORN: 7/27/1950 • PLAYED FOR VARSITY: 1969–1971

Reggie McKenzie and teammate Dan Dierdorf were the building blocks of Michigan's great offensive line in the late 1960s and early 1970s. McKenzie was quick enough to pull back from his position and block for plays aimed at the sidelines.

TYRONE WHEATLEY   Running Back

- BORN: 1/19/1972
- PLAYED FOR VARSITY: 1991–1994

Tyrone Wheatley was a popular and respected team player. His power and speed made him the best running back in the Big Ten during the early 1990s. He was the conference rushing and scoring champion in 1992, and then was named MVP of the Rose Bowl.

JAKE LONG   Offensive Lineman

- BORN: 5/9/1985
- PLAYED FOR VARSITY: 2004–2007

Jake Long was a rock-solid blocker for the Wolverines. He was the Big Ten's Offensive Lineman of the Year in 2006 and 2007. Long was also a two-time team captain. Fewer than a dozen Wolverines had earned that honor.

LEFT: Ron Johnson
RIGHT: Jake Long

On the Sidelines

The history of Michigan football might have been different if it weren't for a silly rule at another school. In 1901, Stanford University in California decided that all its coaches had to be former students. That forced coach Fielding Yost to pack his bags and look for another job. The Wolverines hired Yost, and he turned Michigan into a football powerhouse.

Yost always told his players to hurry up in practice. His nickname became—what else?—"Hurry-Up." Yost led the Wolverines to six national championships before he became the school's **athletic director**. Several great coaches followed Yost, including Harry Kipke, Fritz Crisler, and Bennie Oosterbaan. Bo Schembechler was the best of those who came after Yost. He arrived in Michigan in 1969 and guided the Wolverines to 13 Big Ten championships in 21 seasons.

In 1995, Michigan made Lloyd Carr its head coach. Schembechler had hired Carr 15 years earlier as an assistant coach. In 1997, Carr led the Wolverines to the national championship.

Bo Schembechler shouts instructions to his players during the 1990 Rose Bowl. He was one of the greatest coaches in school history.

Rivals

egend has it that Michigan students introduced football to Notre Dame in 1887. The two schools have had a fierce rivalry ever since. Michigan has won the most games of any college, and Notre Dame has won the second most. The two schools have

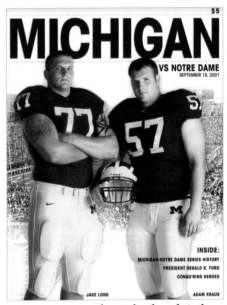

played many exciting games over the years. The Wolverines took the first eight games they played against the Fighting Irish. In 2007, Michigan embarrassed Notre Dame in a 38–0 blowout.

Michigan's greatest rival is Ohio State. Since the 1930s, these two teams have faced off in the final game of the Big Ten season. Often, a championship is on the line. From 1972 to 1981, the contest decided which team would play in the Rose Bowl.

In 1969, Bo Schembechler coached his first game against Ohio State. He had once been an assistant to Woody Hayes, the coach of the Buckeyes. Schembechler desperately wanted a victory over

his former boss. The Wolverines delivered for him, as Michigan won 24–12. The victory was even sweeter because it ended Ohio State's 22-game winning streak.

Quarterback Rick Leach holds a special place in the hearts of Michigan fans. Starting in 1976, Leach led the Wolverines to three wins in a row over the Buckeyes. The Michigan defense stood strong, too. It didn't allow a touchdown in any of those games.

LEFT: Jake Long and Adam Kraus are all business on the cover of Michigan's program for the 2007 Notre Dame game.
ABOVE: Rick Leach of the Wolverines signals a touchdown during Michigan's win over Ohio State in 1977.

One Great Day

In the early days of college football, voting for the national champion took place after the regular season. Bowl games were not counted. In 1947, Michigan fans believed that the Wolverines

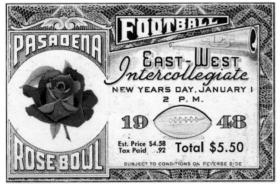

were the nation's top team. The voters disagreed. They named Notre Dame as the national champion.

The Wolverines could not wait for the Rose Bowl. They would play USC. This was their chance to prove what a great team they were. Notre Dame had just beaten the Trojans 38–7. Since the Wolverines and the Fighting Irish did not play each other in 1947, Michigan's game against USC would be the best way to compare the two.

Michigan's defense was ***extraordinary***. The Trojans struggled for every yard they gained. Meanwhile, the Wolverines were having an easy time on offense. Bob Chappuis, Bump Elliott, and Jack Wiesenburger ran wild against USC. Their fakes completely fooled

the defense. The Wolverines rushed for three touchdowns and passed for four more. The final score was 49–0.

After the game, the Associated Press took a special vote to see if sportswriters had changed their minds about the top team in the land. Michigan was declared the "unofficial" national champion by a vote of 226 to 119.

LEFT: A ticket stub from the 1948 Rose Bowl.
ABOVE: The Wolverines power into the end zone during their 49–0 blowout of USC.

It Really Happened

There is not much love for Michigan football players in Columbus, Ohio. Every other year, the Wolverines are reminded of this when they take the field for their game at Ohio State. More than 100,000 Buckeye fans are quick to boo anything Michigan does well.

In 1940, Tom Harmon led the Wolverines into Columbus. Harmon was a terrific athlete and a very nice young man. Many were surprised that he had not won the Heisman Trophy in 1939. As Harmon prepared for his final contest against the Buckeyes, everyone in Ohio Stadium knew that he had to have a great game to claim the Heisman.

For much of the game, the fans screamed in agony. Every time Harmon touched the football, he seemed to make a long run or throw, or break up a pass on defense. Michigan began to build a lead, while the Buckeyes could not reach the end zone.

Harmon ended up running for 139 yards and two touchdowns. He completed 11 of 12 passes for two more touchdowns. He also intercepted three passes. Harmon even kicked four **extra points**.

As the clock ran down on Michigan's 40–0 victory, the strangest thing happened. The fans rose to their feet and began to clap for

Tom Harmon breaks free for a big gain against Ohio State in 1939.
A year later, he had another great game against the Buckeyes.

Harmon. Soon it became a thunderous **ovation**. They were saying *thank you* to a great player who played a great final game against their beloved Buckeyes.

Team Spirit

A wolverine can be mean, scary, and tough. That's why Michigan named its athletic teams after the animal. But there actually are no wolverines in the state. Long ago, trappers sold the furs of wolverines at trading posts in Michigan. In 1927, the team tried to make two wolverines into *mascots*. They were so nasty that they had to be set loose after the season.

Other team traditions have lasted longer, including the team's fight song—"The Victors"—which was written in 1898. That was the same year that the school started its marching band. Today, the Michigan Band has more than 200 musicians. They lead students from *campus* to the stadium on game days.

Nothing shows Michigan's team spirit like the huge banner that reads "GO BLUE." It hangs above the entrance to the field. When the Wolverines rush out of the locker room, they meet up with the cheerleaders and everyone jumps to touch the banner. The first time a freshman taps the banner, it is a special thrill.

The Michigan Band performs for students and other fans during the 2007 season.

Timeline

At the end of each college season, the best teams are invited to play in special "Bowl" games, such as the Rose Bowl, **Orange Bowl**, and **Sugar Bowl**. Bowl games usually take place in January, but they count in the final rankings of the previous season. That means the top team in 2007 wasn't decided until early 2008. In this timeline, bowl games are listed in the year they were held.

1901
The Wolverines win their first national championship.

1879
The Wolverines play their first game.

1940
Tom Harmon wins the Heisman Trophy.

1948
Michigan wins the Rose Bowl in a 49–0 blowout.

A souvenir blanket from the earliest days of Michigan football.

A button celebrating Michigan's national championship in 1997.

1974
Michigan wins its fourth Big Ten title in a row.

1997
Michigan wins its 10th national championship.

1965
Michigan defeats Oregon State University 34–7 in the Rose Bowl.

1991
Erick Anderson wins the **Butkus Award**.

2006
Alan Branch is voted First Team **All-Big Ten**.

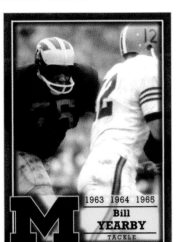

Bill Yearby, a star for the 1965 Wolverines.

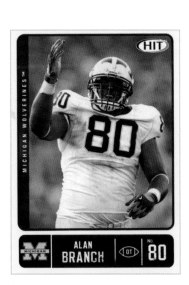

Alan Branch

Fun Facts

RIDING THE PINE

The Wolverines are so talented that sometimes a great player can't get off the bench. Future NFL superstar Tom Brady didn't become Michigan's regular starting quarterback until his senior year.

JUG HANDLERS

When Michigan plays Minnesota, the winner gets to keep the Little Brown Jug for a year. This tradition started in 1903, which makes the jug one of the oldest sports "trophies" in the world.

COMEBACK!

In a 2003 game, Michigan trailed Minnesota by three touchdowns in the fourth quarter. Suddenly the Wolverines could do no wrong—they scored 31 points to win 38–35. It was the biggest comeback in school history.

THAT 70s SHOW

During the 1970s, the Wolverines had a 96–10–3 record. No team in college football was better during the *decade*.

LORD OF THE RING

After playing for the Wolverines in 1942, Bob Chappuis left to fight in World War II. When his plane was shot down over Italy in 1945, he had one thing on his mind: "You can have everything, but you can't have my Michigan ring!"

CENTER OF ATTENTION

After the 1934 season, the Michigan players voted center Gerald Ford as their MVP. Forty years later, Ford became president of the United States.

TALK TO TIM

Michigan's best running back in the mid-1990s was Tshimanga Biakabutuka. It was a hard name to pronounce so everyone called him "Tim." Biakabatuka had no problem with foreign words—he spoke five different languages!

LEFT: Tom Brady fires a pass for the Wolverines.
ABOVE: Gerald Ford

For the Record

 he great Wolverines teams and players have left their marks on the record books. These are the "best of the best" …

WOLVERINES AWARD WINNERS

HEISMAN TROPHY
TOP COLLEGE PLAYER

Tom Harmon	1940
Desmond Howard	1991
Charles Woodson	1997

MAXWELL AWARD
TOP COLLEGE PLAYER

Tom Harmon	1940
Desmond Howard	1991

WALTER CAMP AWARD
TOP COLLEGE PLAYER

Desmond Howard	1991
Charles Woodson	1997

DOAK WALKER AWARD
TOP RUNNING BACK

Chris Perry	2003

RIMINGTON AWARD
TOP CENTER

David Baas	2004*

* Shared this award with another player.

FRED BILETNIKOFF AWARD
TOP RECEIVER

Braylon Edwards	2004

JIM THORPE AWARD
TOP DEFENSIVE BACK

Charles Woodson	1997

VINCE LOMBARDI AWARD
TOP LINEMAN

LaMarr Woodley	2006

DICK BUTKUS AWARD
TOP LINEBACKER

Erick Anderson	1991

BRONKO NAGURSKI AWARD
TOP DEFENSIVE PLAYER

Charles Woodson	1997

CHUCK BEDNARIK AWARD
TOP DEFENSIVE PLAYER

Charles Woodson	1997

TED HENDRICKS AWARD
TOP DEFENSIVE END

LaMarr Woodley	2006

Chris Perry

LaMarr Woodley

A pennant celebrating Michigan's national championship in 1948.

WOLVERINES ACHIEVEMENTS

ACHIEVEMENT	YEAR	ACHIEVEMENT	YEAR
Big Ten Champions	1898	National Champions	1948
Big Ten Champions	1901*	Big Ten Champions	1949*
National Champions	1901	Big Ten Champions	1950
Big Ten Champions	1902	Big Ten Champions	1964
National Champions	1902	Big Ten Champions	1969*
Big Ten Champions	1903*	Big Ten Champions	1971
National Champions	1903	Big Ten Champions	1972*
Big Ten Champions	1904*	Big Ten Champions	1973*
National Champions	1904	Big Ten Champions	1974*
Big Ten Champions	1906*	Big Ten Champions	1976*
Big Ten Champions	1918*	Big Ten Champions	1977*
National Champions	1918	Big Ten Champions	1978*
Big Ten Champions	1922*	Big Ten Champions	1980
Big Ten Champions	1923*	Big Ten Champions	1982
National Champions	1923*	Big Ten Champions	1986*
Big Ten Champions	1925	Big Ten Champions	1988
Big Ten Champions	1926*	Big Ten Champions	1989
Big Ten Champions	1930*	Big Ten Champions	1990*
Big Ten Champions	1931*	Big Ten Champions	1991
Big Ten Champions	1932*	Big Ten Champions	1992
National Champions	1932	Big Ten Champions	1997
Big Ten Champions	1933*	National Champions	1997*
National Champions	1933	Big Ten Champions	1998*
Big Ten Champions	1943*	Big Ten Champions	2000*
Big Ten Champions	1947	Big Ten Champions	2003
Big Ten Champions	1948	Big Ten Champions	2004*

* *Shared this honor with another school.*

Michigan's 1997 pocket schedule hints at great things to come for the team.

The Big Ten

The University of Michigan is a member of the Big Ten Conference, the oldest college sports conference in America. Over the years, the Big Ten actually expanded to 11 teams. These are the Wolverines' neighbors …

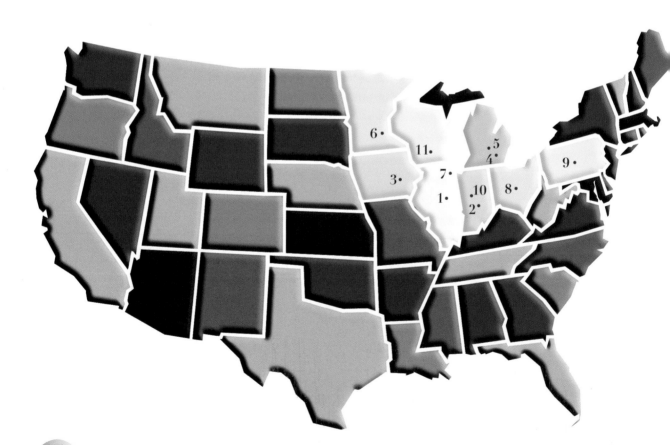

THE BIG TEN

1 University of Illinois Fighting Illini
Urbana-Champaign, Illinois

2 Indiana University Hoosiers
Bloomington, Indiana

3 University of Iowa Hawkeyes
Iowa City, Iowa

4 University of Michigan Wolverines
Ann Arbor, Michigan

5 Michigan State University Spartans
East Lansing, Michigan

6 University of Minnesota Golden Gophers
Minneapolis and Saint Paul, Minnesota

7 Northwestern University Wildcats
Evanston, Illinois

8 Ohio State University Buckeyes
Columbus, Ohio

9 Pennsylvania State University Nittany Lions*
University Park, Pennsylvania

10 Purdue University Boilermakers
West Lafayette, Indiana

11 University of Wisconsin Badgers
Madison, Wisconsin

* Penn State joined the Big Ten in 1993.

The College Game

College football may look like the same game you see NFL teams play on Sundays, but there are some important differences. The first is that most college games take place on Saturday. This has been true for more than 100 years. Below are several other differences between college and pro football.

CLASS NOTES

College players are younger than NFL players. They are student-athletes who have graduated from high school and now play on their college's varsity team, which is the highest level of competition. Most are between the ages of 18 and 22.

College players are allowed to compete for four seasons. Each year is given a different name or "class"—freshman (first year), sophomore (second year), junior (third year), and senior (fourth year). Players who are unable to play for the varsity can remain in the same class for an extra year. This is called "red-shirting." These players are still students and must attend classes during their extra year.

RULE BOOK

There are several differences between the rules in college football and the NFL. Here are the important ones: 1) In college, a play ends as soon as the ball carrier's knee touches the ground, even if he slips or dives. In the NFL, a player must be tackled. 2) In college, a player catching the ball near the sideline must have one foot in bounds for the reception to count. In the NFL, a player must have both feet in bounds. 3) Since 1996, tie games in college have been decided by a special overtime period. Each team is given a chance to score from its opponent's 25-yard line. In the NFL, the first team to score in overtime is the winner.

WHO'S NUMBER 1?

How is the national champion of college football decided? Each week during the season, teams are ranked from best to worst in several different polls of coaches and sportswriters. These rankings are based on many factors, including a team's record and the level of competition that it has played. At the end of the year, the two top-ranked teams play each other. The winner is declared the national champion. This tradition started in 1998 when college football began using the Bowl Championship Series. Prior to that year, the top two teams did not always face each other. Sometimes, that made it very difficult to decide which school was the best.

CONFERENCE CALL

Most colleges are members of athletic conferences. Each conference represents a different part of the country. For example, the Atlantic Coast Conference is made up of teams from up and down the East Coast. Teams that belong to a conference are required to play a certain number of games against the other teams in their conference. At the end of the year, the team with the best record is crowned conference champion (unless the league holds a championship game). Teams also play schools from outside their conference. Wins and losses in those games do not count in the conference standings. However, they are very important to a team's national ranking.

BOWL GAMES

Bowl games—such as the Rose Bowl, Sugar Bowl, and Orange Bowl—are extra games played at the end of each season. Bowl games give fans a chance to see the best teams from around the country play one another. These games are scheduled during the Christmas and New Year's holiday season, so students are free to travel to the cities where bowl games are played. There are now more than 25 bowl games.

Since 1998, the BCS has selected the nation's very best teams and carefully matched them in a handful of bowl games. The BCS chooses the champions of major conferences, as well as other schools with talented teams. The two top-ranked teams meet in the BCS title game for the national championship.

Glossary

FOOTBALL WORDS TO KNOW

ALL-AMERICAN—A college player voted as the best at his position.

ALL-BIG TEN—A player voted as the best at his position in the Big Ten Conference.

BACKFIELD—The players who line up in back of the line of scrimmage. On offense, the quarterback and running backs are in the backfield.

BLOCKING—Protection of the ball carrier by his teammates.

BOWL CHAMPIONSHIP SERIES (BCS)—The system used by college football to select the best two teams to play for the national championship each season. Before the BCS came along, the national championship was unofficial, and more than one team often claimed they were the best.

BUTKUS AWARD—The award given each year to college football's best linebacker.

DRAFTED—Chosen from a group of the best college players. The NFL draft is held each spring.

EXTRA POINTS—Kicks worth one point attempted after touchdowns.

FIELD GOALS—Goals from the field, kicked over the crossbar and between the goal posts. A field goal is worth three points

HEISMAN TROPHY—The award given each year to the best player in college football.

INTERCEPTIONS—Passes that are caught by the defensive team.

LINE OF SCRIMMAGE—The imaginary line that separates the offense and defense before each play begins.

MOST VALUABLE PLAYER (MVP)—The award given to the top player in each bowl game and an honor given each year by some conferences.

NATIONAL FOOTBALL LEAGUE (NFL)—The league that started in 1920 and is still operating today.

ORANGE BOWL—The annual bowl game played in Miami, Florida. The first Orange Bowl was played in 1935.

PROFESSIONAL—A player or team that plays a sport for money. College players are not paid, so they are considered "amateurs."

ROSE BOWL—The annual bowl game played in Pasadena, California. The Tournament of Roses Parade takes place before the game. The first Rose Bowl was played in 1902.

ROSTER—The list of a team's active players.

SACK—A tackle of the quarterback behind the line of scrimmage.

SECONDARY—The part of the defense made up by the cornerbacks and safeties.

SUGAR BOWL—The annual bowl game played in New Orleans, Louisiana. The first Sugar Bowl was played in 1935.

OTHER WORDS TO KNOW

ATHLETIC DIRECTOR—The person in charge of a college's sports program.

CAMPUS—The grounds and buildings of a college.

CENTURY—A period of 100 years.

COMEBACK—The process of catching up from behind, or making up a large deficit.

COMPETITIVE—Having a strong desire to win.

DECADE—A period of 10 years; also specific periods, such as the 1950s.

ERAS—Periods of time in history.

EXTRAORDINARY—Unusual, or unusually talented.

IMAGINATIVE—Creative.

MASCOTS—Animals or people believed to bring a group good luck.

OVATION—A long, loud cheer.

RIVAL—Extremely emotional competitor.

TAILBONE—The bone that protects the base of the spine.

TRADITIONS—Beliefs or customs that are handed down from generation to generation.

UNDEFEATED—Without a loss.

Places to Go

ON THE ROAD

UNIVERSITY OF MICHIGAN
1 East Stadium Boulevard
Ann Arbor, Michigan 48104
(313) 936-9345

COLLEGE FOOTBALL HALL OF FAME
111 South St. Joseph Street
South Bend, Indiana 46601
(800) 440-3263

ON THE WEB

THE UNIVERSITY OF MICHIGAN WOLVERINES   www.mgoblue.com/football/
  • *Learn more about the Wolverines*

BIG TEN CONFERENCE   bigten.cstv.com
  • *Learn more about the Big Ten teams*

COLLEGE FOOTBALL HALL OF FAME   www.collegefootball.org
  • *Learn more about college football*

ON THE BOOKSHELF

To learn more about the sport of football, look for these books at your library or bookstore:

  • Kaufman, Gabriel. *Football in the Big Ten*. New York, New York: Rosen Central, 2008.
  • DeCock, Luke. *Great Teams in College Football History*. Chicago, Illinois: Raintree, 2006.
  • Yuen, Kevin. *The 10 Most Intense College Football Rivalries*. New York, New York: Franklin Watts, 2008.

Index

PAGE NUMBERS IN **BOLD** REFER TO ILLUSTRATIONS.

Anderson, Erick 37, 40

Baas, David 11, 40

Biakabatuka, Tim 39

Blott, Jack 6

Brady, Tom 38, **38**

Branch, Alan 37, **37**

Carr, Lloyd 27

Carter, Anthony 9, 20

Chappuis, Bob **17**, 22, 30, 39

Crisler, Fritz 14, 17, 27

Dierdorf, Dan 25

Edwards, Braylon 11, 23, **23**, 40

Edwards, Stan 23

Elliott, Bump 30

Elliott, Jumbo 9

Elliott, Pete 17

Ford, Gerald 13, 39, **39**

Friedman, Benny **14**, 20, **20**

Grange, Red 22

Griese, Brian 9, 18, **19**

Harbaugh, Jim 9, 21

Harmon, Tom 6, 13, 20,
32, 33, **33**, 36, 40

Hart, Mike.......................**10**, **15**

Hayes, Woody 28

Henne, Chad **10**

Hernstein, Albert 16

Heston, Willie 16, **16**, 22

Howard, Chris 18

Howard, Desmond 9, **9**, 21, **21**, 40

Johnson, Ron 7, 24, **24**

Kipke, Harry 6, 27

Kramer, Ron 7, **7**, 13, 24

Kraus, Adam **28**

Leach, Rick 9, 23, 29, **29**

Long, Jake.................**10**, 25, **25**, 28

Lytle, Rob 9

Mack, Tom 7

Maentz, Tom 7, **7**

McKenzie, Reggie 25

Newman, Harry 6, **6**

O'Neal, Calvin 9

Oosterbaan, Bennie 13, 17,
22, **22**, 27

Perry, Chris 11, 40, **40**

Rifenburg, Dick 17

Rodriguez, Rich 11

Schembechler, Bo 7, **26**, 27, 28

Snow, Neil 16

Steele, Glen 18

Streets, Tai 18

Timberlake, Bob 7

Tuman, Jerame 18

Volk, Rick 7

Weeks, Harrison 16

Wheatley, Tyrone 25

Wiesenburger, Jack 30

Wistert, Albert 13, 24

Wistert, Alvin 13, 24

Wistert, Francis 13, 24

Woodley, LaMarr 11, 40, **40**

Woodson, Charles **8**, 9,
18, **18**, 21, 40

Woolfolk, Butch 23

Yearby, Bill 7, **37**

Yost, Fielding 6, 16, 27

About the Author

MARK STEWART has written more than 30 books on football players and teams, and over 100 sports books for kids. He has also interviewed dozens of athletes, politicians, and celebrities. Although Mark grew up in New York City, as a young fan he loved Big Ten football. He rooted for Michigan's stars from the 1960s and 1970s, including Ron Johnson, who became one of his favorite players. Mark comes from a family of writers. His grandfather was Sunday Editor of *The New York Times* and his mother was Articles Editor for *Ladies' Home Journal* and *McCall's*. Mark became interested in sports during lazy summer days spent at the Connecticut home of his father's godfather, sportswriter John R. Tunis. Mark is a graduate of Duke University, with a degree in History. He lives with his wife Sarah, and daughters Mariah and Rachel, overlooking Sandy Hook, New Jersey.